Advent Cookies Around the World: A Global Gastronomic Journey

S.R. Moore

Published by S.R. Moore, 2023.

While every precaution has been taken in the preparation of this book, the publisher assumes no responsibility for errors or omissions, or for damages resulting from the use of the information contained herein.

ADVENT COOKIES AROUND THE WORLD: A GLOBAL GASTRONOMIC JOURNEY

First edition. November 28, 2023.

ISBN: 979-8224647286

Written by S.R. Moore.

Also by S.R. Moore

Mysteries of Lavender Lane
The Secret of Lavender Lane
The Book Club Conspiracy
The Mosaic Murders

Standalone
Pizza Artistry: The Canvas of Flavor
Brews & Bites: A Beer Cheese Revolution
Souper Fusion: A Globetrotter's Culinary Journey in a Bowl
Slices of Heaven: Sandwiches Redefined for the Modern Foodie
Advent Cookies Around the World: A Global Gastronomic Journey
Pasta for the Senses
Shamrock & Spoon: Modern Irish Cooking for Every Occasion

Table of Contents

Introduction

Introducing "Advent Cookies Around the World: A Global Gastronomic Journey" – a delightful and diverse cookbook that takes you on an enchanting culinary adventure through the traditions of Advent cookies from around the world. In this remarkable collection, we celebrate the rich tapestry of global holiday flavors, bringing you 25 meticulously crafted recipes that encapsulate the essence of each country's unique culture and history.

This cookbook is a testament to the unifying power of food, demonstrating how similar ingredients like butter, sugar, and flour can be transformed into an array of captivating cookies, each with its own story to tell. Whether you're a seasoned baker or just beginning your culinary journey, these recipes offer a delightful way to explore new flavors and traditions, making your holiday season truly special.

With each recipe, you'll embark on a journey to discover the origins, customs, and unique twists that make these Advent cookies so extraordinary. From the delicate Madeleines of France to the aromatic Almond Briouats of Morocco, we'll dive into the heartwarming stories behind these sweet creations.

This cookbook doesn't just stop at recipes; it's also filled with helpful tips, optional variations, and substitution suggestions to cater to your preferences and dietary needs. Whether you're looking to experiment with different fillings, explore new spice blends, or adapt recipes to accommodate allergies, we've got you covered.

So, join us on this flavorful expedition as we traverse continents and traditions, one cookie at a time. Whether you're baking these delectable treats for your own enjoyment or sharing them with loved ones, "Advent

Cookies Around the World" is your passport to a holiday season filled with global gastronomic delights. Get ready to create cherished memories, one batch of cookies at a time.

Essential Tools, Utensils, and Equipment:

Mixing Bowls: Various sizes of mixing bowls for combining ingredients and preparing dough.

Whisk: For mixing wet ingredients, especially in recipes that require eggs.

Hand or Stand Mixer: Useful for creaming butter and sugar or whipping up fluffy batters.

Measuring Cups and Spoons: For accurate measurement of dry and liquid ingredients.

Baking Sheets: To bake the cookies. Consider using parchment paper or silicone baking mats for easy cleanup.

Cookie Cutters: If your recipes require shaping the cookies into specific forms.

Rolling Pin: For rolling out dough to the desired thickness.

Spatula: For transferring cookies from baking sheets and handling delicate dough.

Cooling Rack: To allow cookies to cool evenly and prevent them from becoming soggy.

Pastry Brush: For brushing cookies with melted butter or other coatings.

Mini Muffin Tin: Required for recipes like Hertzoggies (South Africa).

Filo Pastry Sheets: For recipes like Moroccan Almond Briouats.

Zester or Microplane: To zest citrus fruits for added flavor.

Baking Powder: Necessary for recipes that require leavening.

Parchment Paper: To line baking sheets and prevent cookies from sticking.

Plastic Wrap: For chilling dough and keeping it fresh.

Cookie Scoop: Optional but useful for uniform cookie sizes.

Pantry Essentials:

Flour: All-purpose flour is the primary type used in most recipes.

Sugar: Granulated sugar, powdered sugar, and brown sugar are common sweeteners.

Butter: Unsalted butter is generally preferred for baking.

Eggs: Large eggs are typically used in cookie recipes.

Baking Powder: For leavening cookies.

Spices: Common spices include cinnamon, nutmeg, cloves, and ginger.

Vanilla Extract: Adds flavor to many cookie recipes.

Ground Nuts: Such as almonds, walnuts, or pecans, used in various recipes.

Jam or Preserves: Often used as fillings in certain cookies.

Fruit Zest: Such as lemon or orange zest for added flavor.

Cornstarch: Used in some shortbread-style cookies.

Matcha Green Tea Powder: For matcha-flavored cookies (optional).

Anise Extract: For recipes that require anise flavor (optional).

Honey: For drizzling on cookies like Almond Briouats (Morocco).

Orange Blossom Water: Used in Moroccan Almond Briouats (optional).

Filberts or Almond Meal: For recipes that require ground nuts.

Jam or Fruit Preserves: For filling cookies like Hertzoggies (South Africa).

Sesame Seeds: Used as a garnish for some cookies.

Cornstarch: Used in some shortbread-style cookies.

Chocolate Chips: For recipes that call for chocolate.

Saffron Threads: For added flavor and color (optional).

Dried Fruits: For recipes that include fruits like figs or apricots (optional).

Cocoa Powder: For chocolate-flavored cookies (optional).

Anise Seeds: For recipes that require anise flavor (optional).

Ground Cardamom: Used in some recipes for flavor (optional).

Before you start baking, review the specific recipes you plan to make and ensure you have all the necessary ingredients and equipment on hand. This will help make your cookie-baking experience smooth and enjoyable.

Fundamental Cooking Techniques

Creaming Butter and Sugar:

Technique: Beat softened butter and sugar together until light and fluffy.

Tip: Use room temperature butter for easier creaming and better texture.

Mixing Dry Ingredients:

Technique: Sift or whisk dry ingredients (flour, baking powder, spices) together to ensure even distribution.

Tip: Measure dry ingredients accurately using dry measuring cups and leveling them off.

Incorporating Eggs:

Technique: Add eggs one at a time, mixing well after each addition to prevent curdling.

Tip: Use large eggs at room temperature for better emulsification.

Rolling Dough:

Technique: Roll out cookie dough on a floured surface to the specified thickness.

Tip: Use rolling pin guides or rolling pin rings to maintain even thickness.

Shaping and Cutting Cookies:

Technique: Use cookie cutters or shape dough into desired forms.

Tip: Dip cookie cutters in flour to prevent sticking.

Handling Filo Pastry Sheets:

Technique: When using filo pastry, work quickly and keep unused sheets covered with a damp cloth to prevent drying out.

Baking Cookies:

Technique: Preheat the oven to the specified temperature and use an oven thermometer for accuracy.

Tip: Rotate baking sheets halfway through baking for even browning.

Cooling Cookies:

Technique: Allow cookies to cool on a wire rack to prevent them from becoming soggy.

Drizzling with Honey or Icing:

Technique: Use a spoon or pastry brush to evenly drizzle honey or icing over cookies.

Tip: Warm honey slightly to make it easier to drizzle.

Dusting with Powdered Sugar:

Technique: Use a fine sieve or sifter to evenly dust cookies with powdered sugar.

Tip: Wait until cookies are completely cool before dusting to prevent clumping.

Filling Cookies:

Technique: When filling cookies with jam or preserves, use a small spoon or pastry bag for precision.

Tip: Be sure to leave a small border around the edges to prevent filling from oozing out.

Flattening Dough:

Technique: Use the bottom of a glass or the palm of your hand to flatten cookie dough evenly.

Zesting Citrus:

Technique: Use a microplane or fine grater to zest citrus fruits, being careful not to include the bitter white pith.

Handling Shortbread Dough:

Technique: Shortbread dough can be crumbly; press it firmly into molds or tartlet shells.

Using Matcha Green Tea Powder:

Technique: Matcha powder should be sifted before use to remove lumps.

Tip: Use high-quality matcha for the best flavor and color.

Making Fillings:

Technique: When making fillings like almond paste or nut mixtures, ensure even mixing for consistent flavor.

Brushing with Butter:

Technique: Use a pastry brush to apply melted butter evenly to cookies before baking.

Tip: Use clarified butter for a cleaner appearance.

Chilling Dough:

Technique: Refrigerate dough as specified in the recipe to firm it up for easier handling.

Handling Filo Pastry Sheets:

Technique: Keep filo pastry covered with a damp cloth to prevent drying out, and work quickly to avoid tearing.

Slicing Biscotti:

Technique: Use a sharp knife to slice biscotti diagonally while they are still slightly warm.

Creating Designs:

Technique: When making shaped cookies, use decorating tools or icing pens for intricate designs.

Garnishing:

Technique: Sprinkle or drizzle garnishes like chopped nuts, toasted sesame seeds, or extra spices with precision.

Sealing Filled Cookies:

Technique: Ensure that filled cookies are well-sealed to prevent filling from leaking during baking.

Storing Cookies:

Tip: Store cookies in an airtight container to maintain freshness and prevent them from becoming stale.

Experiment and Have Fun:

Tip: Don't be afraid to experiment with different flavor variations and substitutions to create your unique twist on the recipes.

Remember that practice makes perfect, so don't be discouraged if your first batch isn't picture-perfect. Baking is an enjoyable learning experience, and with each attempt, you'll refine your skills and create delicious Advent cookies to share with friends and family.

Mexican Wedding Cookies (Mexico)

Ingredients:

1 cup unsalted butter, softened

1/2 cup powdered sugar

2 teaspoons pure vanilla extract

2 cups all-purpose flour

1 cup finely chopped pecans or almonds

Additional powdered sugar for dusting

Instructions:

Preheat your oven to 325°F (160°C). Line a baking sheet with parchment paper.

In a mixing bowl, cream together the softened butter and powdered sugar until light and fluffy.

Stir in the vanilla extract, then gradually add the flour and chopped nuts, mixing until the dough comes together.

Shape the dough into 1-inch balls and place them on the prepared baking sheet.

Bake for about 15-20 minutes, or until the cookies are just beginning to turn golden.

Remove the cookies from the oven and let them cool for a few minutes.

Roll the warm cookies in powdered sugar and place them on a wire rack to cool completely.

Once cooled, roll them in powdered sugar again for a sweet finish.

Origin: Mexican Wedding Cookies, also known as Polvorones, are a popular treat at Mexican weddings and other celebrations. Their crumbly, melt-in-your-mouth texture makes them a beloved holiday cookie.

Preparation Time: 20 minutes

Cooking Time: 15-20 minutes

Yield: About 36 cookies

Optional Variations or Substitutions: You can experiment with different types of nuts, such as almonds or walnuts, for a unique flavor. You can also add a pinch of cinnamon for a subtle spice.

Tips and Notes for Success: Make sure the cookies are completely cooled before rolling them in powdered sugar for the best texture.

Lebkuchen (Germany)

Ingredients:

2 1/4 cups all-purpose flour

1/2 cup ground almonds

1/2 cup candied orange peel, finely chopped

1/4 cup candied lemon peel, finely chopped

1/2 cup honey

1/2 cup molasses

1/4 cup unsalted butter

1/2 cup granulated sugar

2 teaspoons ground cinnamon

1/2 teaspoon ground cloves

1/2 teaspoon ground ginger

1/2 teaspoon baking soda

1/4 teaspoon salt

1 egg, beaten

Icing sugar for dusting

Instructions:

In a large bowl, combine the flour, ground almonds, candied orange peel, and candied lemon peel.

In a saucepan, heat the honey, molasses, butter, granulated sugar, ground spices, baking soda, and salt. Stir until the sugar and butter are melted. Remove from heat and let it cool slightly.

Pour the honey mixture into the dry ingredients and mix until a stiff dough forms. Add the beaten egg and mix until well combined.

Cover the dough and refrigerate for at least 1 hour or until firm.

Preheat your oven to 350°F (175°C). Line a baking sheet with parchment paper.

Roll out the dough on a floured surface to about 1/4-inch thickness. Use cookie cutters to cut out desired shapes.

Place the cookies on the prepared baking sheet and bake for 12-15 minutes or until they are lightly golden.

Remove the cookies from the oven and let them cool completely. Dust with icing sugar before serving.

Origin: Lebkuchen is a traditional German Christmas cookie with roots dating back to the 13th century. These spiced and honey-sweetened cookies are a cherished part of German holiday celebrations.

Preparation Time: 30 minutes (plus chilling time)

Cooking Time: 12-15 minutes

Yield: About 24 cookies

Optional Variations or Substitutions: You can add chopped nuts or dried fruits to the dough for extra flavor and texture. Some recipes also include a chocolate glaze on top.

Tips and Notes for Success: The dough can be sticky, so make sure to flour your work surface and rolling pin when rolling it out.

Alfajores (Argentina)

Ingredients:

1 3/4 cups all-purpose flour

1/2 cup cornstarch

1 teaspoon baking powder

1/2 teaspoon baking soda

1/4 teaspoon salt

1/2 cup unsalted butter, softened

1/4 cup granulated sugar

3 egg yolks

1 teaspoon pure vanilla extract

Dulce de leche (for filling)

Shredded coconut (for rolling)

Instructions:

In a bowl, sift together the flour, cornstarch, baking powder, baking soda, and salt.

In another bowl, cream the softened butter and sugar until light and fluffy.

Add the egg yolks and vanilla extract to the butter mixture, beating until well combined.

Gradually add the dry ingredients to the wet ingredients, mixing until a soft dough forms.

Divide the dough in half and shape each half into a disc. Wrap in plastic wrap and refrigerate for at least 1 hour.

Preheat your oven to 350°F (175°C). Line a baking sheet with parchment paper.

Roll out one disc of dough on a floured surface to about 1/4-inch thickness. Use a round cookie cutter to cut out cookies.

Place the cookies on the prepared baking sheet and bake for 10-12 minutes, or until they are lightly golden.

Remove from the oven and let them cool completely.

Spread a layer of dulce de leche on the bottom of one cookie and sandwich it with another cookie. Roll the edges in shredded coconut.

Origin: Alfajores are beloved sweet treats in Argentina and many other Latin American countries. These delicate cookies, with their caramel filling and coconut coating, are enjoyed year-round and during the holidays.

Preparation Time: 20 minutes (plus chilling time)

Cooking Time: 10-12 minutes

Yield: About 20 alfajores

Optional Variations or Substitutions: You can use chocolate chips or cocoa powder in the dough for a chocolate twist. Some recipes also dip the finished alfajores in chocolate.

Tips and Notes for Success: Be gentle when handling the cookies after baking, as they can be delicate. Store them in an airtight container to keep them fresh.

Kourabiedes (Greece)

Ingredients:

1 cup unsalted butter, softened

1/2 cup powdered sugar

1 teaspoon pure vanilla extract

2 cups all-purpose flour

1 cup blanched almonds, toasted and finely chopped

Additional powdered sugar for dusting

Instructions:

Preheat your oven to 325°F (160°C). Line a baking sheet with parchment paper.

In a mixing bowl, cream together the softened butter and powdered sugar until light and fluffy.

Stir in the vanilla extract, then gradually add the flour and chopped almonds, mixing until the dough comes together.

Shape the dough into crescent or ball shapes and place them on the prepared baking sheet.

Bake for about 20-25 minutes, or until the cookies are just beginning to turn golden.

Remove the cookies from the oven and let them cool for a few minutes.

While still warm, dust the cookies generously with powdered sugar.

Once cooled, roll them in powdered sugar again for an extra sweet touch.

Origin: Kourabiedes are traditional Greek butter cookies enjoyed during special occasions and holidays like Christmas. Their crumbly, buttery texture and almond flavor make them a favorite among Greeks.

Preparation Time: 20 minutes

Cooking Time: 20-25 minutes

Yield: About 36 cookies

Optional Variations or Substitutions: You can replace the almonds with other nuts like walnuts or pistachios. Some recipes also include a hint of brandy for added flavor.

Tips and Notes for Success: Handle the cookies gently when rolling them in powdered sugar to avoid breaking them. The more powdered sugar, the better!

Pfeffernüsse (Denmark)

Ingredients:

2 cups all-purpose flour

1/2 cup granulated sugar

1/2 cup brown sugar

1/2 teaspoon baking soda

1/4 teaspoon ground black pepper

1/2 teaspoon ground cinnamon

1/4 teaspoon ground cloves

1/4 teaspoon ground nutmeg

1/4 teaspoon ground allspice

1/2 cup unsalted butter, softened

2 large eggs

1/2 teaspoon pure almond extract

Powdered sugar for dusting

Instructions:

In a large bowl, whisk together the flour, granulated sugar, brown sugar, baking soda, and spices.

In another bowl, cream the softened butter until smooth, then add the eggs and almond extract, mixing until well combined.

Gradually add the dry ingredients to the wet ingredients, mixing until a soft dough forms.

Cover the dough and refrigerate for at least 1 hour or until firm.

Preheat your oven to 350°F (175°C). Line a baking sheet with parchment paper.

Roll the dough into small balls (about 1 inch in diameter) and place them on the prepared baking sheet.

Bake for 10-12 minutes, or until the cookies are firm and lightly browned.

Remove from the oven and let them cool on a wire rack.

Once cooled, dust the cookies generously with powdered sugar.

Origin: Pfeffernüsse, which translates to "pepper nuts," are traditional Danish and German Christmas cookies. Despite their name, they are sweet and spiced, with a hint of pepper adding a unique twist to the flavor.

Preparation Time: 20 minutes (plus chilling time)

Cooking Time: 10-12 minutes

Yield: About 36 cookies

Optional Variations or Substitutions: You can add chopped candied ginger or lemon zest for a different flavor profile. Some recipes also drizzle a simple glaze over the cookies for extra sweetness.

Tips and Notes for Success: These cookies are best enjoyed a day or two after baking, as their flavors develop over time. Store them in an airtight container to keep them fresh.

Anzac Biscuits (Australia)

Ingredients:

1 cup rolled oats

1 cup all-purpose flour

1 cup granulated sugar

1/2 cup desiccated coconut

1/2 cup unsalted butter

2 tablespoons golden syrup or honey

1/2 teaspoon baking soda

2 tablespoons boiling water

Instructions:

Preheat your oven to 325°F (160°C). Line a baking sheet with parchment paper.

In a large bowl, combine the rolled oats, flour, sugar, and desiccated coconut.

In a saucepan, melt the butter and golden syrup over low heat.

In a small bowl, dissolve the baking soda in boiling water and add it to the butter mixture.

Pour the wet ingredients over the dry ingredients and stir until well combined.

Drop spoonfuls of the mixture onto the prepared baking sheet, leaving space for spreading.

Bake for 12-15 minutes or until the biscuits are golden brown.

Remove from the oven and let them cool on the baking sheet for a few minutes before transferring them to a wire rack to cool completely.

Origin: Anzac Biscuits have historical significance in Australia and New Zealand. They were originally made and sent to soldiers during World War I by the families at home. The name "Anzac" stands for the Australian and New Zealand Army Corps.

Preparation Time: 15 minutes

Cooking Time: 12-15 minutes

Yield: About 24 biscuits

Optional Variations or Substitutions: You can add chopped nuts or dried fruits to the dough for extra texture and flavor.

Tips and Notes for Success: These biscuits can be quite sticky when hot, so let them cool on the baking sheet for a few minutes before transferring them to a wire rack.

Basler Läckerli (Switzerland)

Ingredients:

2 cups all-purpose flour

1/2 cup ground almonds

1/2 cup candied peel (orange and lemon), finely chopped

1/4 cup honey

1/4 cup granulated sugar

1/4 cup unsalted butter

1/4 teaspoon ground cinnamon

1/4 teaspoon ground cloves

Zest of 1 lemon

1/2 cup powdered sugar

2 tablespoons kirsch (cherry brandy)

Instructions:

Preheat your oven to 350°F (175°C). Line a baking sheet with parchment paper.

In a large bowl, combine the flour, ground almonds, and chopped candied peel.

In a saucepan, heat the honey, granulated sugar, butter, ground cinnamon, ground cloves, and lemon zest. Stir until the sugar and butter are melted.

Pour the honey mixture over the dry ingredients and mix until a dough forms.

Press the dough evenly into the prepared baking sheet.

Bake for 20-25 minutes or until the dough is golden brown.

While still warm, cut the baked dough into diamond-shaped pieces.

In a small bowl, mix the powdered sugar and kirsch to make a glaze. Drizzle the glaze over the warm cookies.

Let the cookies cool completely before removing them from the baking sheet.

Origin: Basler Läckerli is a traditional Swiss gingerbread cookie from the city of Basel. These sweet and slightly spicy cookies have been a cherished holiday treat for centuries.

Preparation Time: 20 minutes

Cooking Time: 20-25 minutes

Yield: About 36 cookies

Optional Variations or Substitutions: You can add chopped nuts or candied ginger for extra flavor and texture. If you don't have kirsch, you can use rum or a similar liqueur for the glaze.

Tips and Notes for Success: It's important to cut the cookies while they are still warm because they become harder as they cool.

Polvorones (Spain)

Ingredients:

2 cups all-purpose flour

1 cup powdered sugar

1 cup ground almonds

1/2 cup unsalted butter, softened

1/2 teaspoon ground cinnamon

1/4 teaspoon ground cloves

1/4 teaspoon ground nutmeg

Zest of 1 lemon

Zest of 1 orange

Instructions:

Preheat your oven to 350°F (175°C). Line a baking sheet with parchment paper.

In a large bowl, combine the flour, powdered sugar, ground almonds, ground spices, and citrus zest.

Add the softened butter to the dry ingredients and mix until the dough comes together.

Shape the dough into small, round cookies and place them on the prepared baking sheet.

Bake for 15-20 minutes or until the cookies are lightly golden.

Remove from the oven and let them cool on the baking sheet for a few minutes before transferring them to a wire rack to cool completely.

Origin: Polvorones are a classic Spanish Christmas cookie, particularly popular in Andalusia. Their name means "powdered" in Spanish, referring to their crumbly and melt-in-your-mouth texture.

Preparation Time: 15 minutes

Cooking Time: 15-20 minutes

Yield: About 24 cookies

Optional Variations or Substitutions: You can add a pinch of ground cloves or cardamom for additional spice. Some recipes use lard instead of butter for a traditional touch.

Tips and Notes for Success: Handle the cookies gently, as they are delicate and can crumble easily when warm.

Vanillekipferl (Austria)

Ingredients:

1 1/2 cups all-purpose flour

1/2 cup ground almonds

1/2 cup granulated sugar

1 cup unsalted butter, cold and cubed

1 teaspoon vanilla extract

1/2 cup powdered sugar

1 tablespoon vanilla sugar (or 1 teaspoon vanilla extract)

Instructions:

Preheat your oven to 350°F (175°C). Line a baking sheet with parchment paper.

In a food processor, combine the flour, ground almonds, and granulated sugar. Add the cold cubed butter and vanilla extract, and pulse until the dough comes together in coarse crumbs.

Shape the dough into crescent-shaped cookies and place them on the prepared baking sheet.

Bake for 10-12 minutes or until the cookies are lightly golden.

While the cookies are still warm, carefully roll them in a mixture of powdered sugar and vanilla sugar (or vanilla extract) to coat them evenly.

Let the cookies cool completely before serving.

Origin: Vanillekipferl, or "vanilla crescents," are a beloved Austrian Christmas cookie. They are famous for their crescent shape and delicate vanilla flavor.

Preparation Time: 20 minutes

Cooking Time: 10-12 minutes

Yield: About 24 cookies

Optional Variations or Substitutions: You can add a pinch of ground cinnamon or cardamom to the dough for a spiced variation.

Tips and Notes for Success: Be gentle when rolling the warm cookies in the powdered sugar to prevent them from breaking.

Biscoitos de Maizena (Brazil)

Ingredients:

1 cup cornstarch (maizena)

1 cup all-purpose flour

1/2 cup granulated sugar

1/2 cup unsalted butter, softened

2 egg yolks

1 teaspoon baking powder

1 teaspoon pure vanilla extract

A pinch of salt

Powdered sugar for dusting

Instructions:

Preheat your oven to 350°F (175°C). Line a baking sheet with parchment paper.

In a large bowl, whisk together the cornstarch, flour, granulated sugar, baking powder, and a pinch of salt.

Add the softened butter, egg yolks, and vanilla extract to the dry ingredients. Mix until a smooth dough forms.

Roll the dough into small balls or shape them into crescents and place them on the prepared baking sheet.

Bake for 15-20 minutes or until the cookies are just set but not browned.

Remove from the oven and let them cool for a few minutes.

Dust the warm cookies generously with powdered sugar.

Once cooled, dust them again with powdered sugar for extra sweetness.

Origin: Biscoitos de Maizena, or cornstarch cookies, are a popular treat in Brazil. They are known for their delicate texture and melt-in-your-mouth quality.

Preparation Time: 20 minutes

Cooking Time: 15-20 minutes

Yield: About 24 cookies

Optional Variations or Substitutions: You can add lemon zest or orange zest for a citrusy twist. Some variations include a tiny amount of baking soda to give the cookies a slight lift.

Tips and Notes for Success: These cookies are fragile, so handle them with care when rolling and dusting with powdered sugar.

Rosettes (Norway)

Ingredients:

2 cups all-purpose flour

2 tablespoons granulated sugar

1/2 teaspoon salt

2 large eggs

1 1/2 cups whole milk

1 teaspoon pure vanilla extract

Vegetable oil for frying

Powdered sugar for dusting

Instructions:

In a mixing bowl, whisk together the flour, granulated sugar, and salt.

In a separate bowl, beat the eggs, then add the milk and vanilla extract, mixing until well combined.

Gradually add the wet ingredients to the dry ingredients, stirring until a smooth batter forms.

Heat about 2 inches of vegetable oil in a deep skillet or pot to 375°F (190°C).

Heat the rosette iron in the hot oil until it sizzles when submerged.

Dip the hot iron into the batter, making sure it covers the iron but doesn't touch the handle.

Quickly return the iron to the hot oil and fry until the rosette is golden brown.

Remove the rosette from the oil and drain on paper towels.

Dust with powdered sugar while still warm.

Repeat the process with the remaining batter.

Origin: Rosettes are a traditional Norwegian Christmas cookie. They are known for their delicate, lacy appearance and are often made using special irons passed down through generations.

Preparation Time: 15 minutes

Cooking Time: Varies (typically about 30 seconds per rosette)

Yield: About 24 rosettes

Optional Variations or Substitutions: You can add a touch of cardamom or cinnamon to the batter for a subtle spice. Some recipes use buttermilk instead of whole milk for a slightly tangy flavor.

Tips and Notes for Success: Be cautious when working with hot oil, and ensure the rosette iron is well-heated to achieve the desired lacy texture.

Kolaczki (Poland)

Ingredients:

2 cups all-purpose flour

1 cup unsalted butter, cold and cubed

8 ounces cream cheese, cold and cubed

1/2 cup powdered sugar

1/2 teaspoon pure vanilla extract

Fruit preserves (apricot, raspberry, or cherry work well)

Powdered sugar for dusting

Instructions:

In a food processor, combine the flour, cold butter, cold cream cheese, powdered sugar, and vanilla extract. Pulse until the dough comes together in a ball.

Divide the dough into two equal portions and shape each into a disk. Wrap in plastic wrap and refrigerate for at least 1 hour or until firm.

Preheat your oven to 350°F (175°C). Line a baking sheet with parchment paper.

Roll out one disk of dough on a floured surface to about 1/8-inch thickness.

Cut the dough into squares or rectangles, about 2 inches in size.

Place a small amount of fruit preserves in the center of each square.

Fold opposite corners of the dough over the filling, creating a pinwheel shape.

Place the filled cookies on the prepared baking sheet and bake for 12-15 minutes or until they are lightly golden.

Remove from the oven and let them cool on a wire rack.

Dust with powdered sugar before serving.

Origin: Kolaczki, also known as kolach or kolache, are popular pastries in Poland and other Eastern European countries. They are often enjoyed during holidays and special occasions.

Preparation Time: 30 minutes (plus chilling time)

Cooking Time: 12-15 minutes

Yield: About 24 kolaczki

Optional Variations or Substitutions: You can use different flavors of fruit preserves or even poppy seed filling for variety.

Tips and Notes for Success: Keep the dough and cream cheese cold for the best texture. Don't overfill the cookies to prevent the filling from leaking out during baking.

Butterkuchen (Sweden)

Ingredients:

1 1/2 cups all-purpose flour

1/2 cup granulated sugar

1 cup unsalted butter, softened

1 egg yolk

1 teaspoon vanilla extract

Raspberry or lingonberry jam

Pearl sugar for sprinkling (optional)

Instructions:

Preheat your oven to 350°F (175°C). Line a baking sheet with parchment paper.

In a mixing bowl, combine the flour and granulated sugar.

Add the softened butter, egg yolk, and vanilla extract to the dry ingredients. Mix until a crumbly dough forms.

Press the dough evenly into the prepared baking sheet.

Spread a layer of raspberry or lingonberry jam over the dough.

Bake for 20-25 minutes or until the edges are lightly golden.

Remove from the oven and let it cool in the pan.

Once cooled, cut into squares or rectangles.

Sprinkle with pearl sugar if desired.

Origin: Butterkuchen, which translates to "butter cake," is a classic Swedish dessert. It is known for its rich, buttery flavor and simple preparation.

Preparation Time: 15 minutes

Cooking Time: 20-25 minutes

Yield: About 20 squares

Optional Variations or Substitutions: You can use your favorite berry jam or even lemon curd as a topping. If pearl sugar is not available, you can use regular granulated sugar for sprinkling.

Tips and Notes for Success: Make sure to press the dough evenly into the pan for even baking and a nice texture.

Ma'amoul (Middle East)

Ingredients:

2 cups fine semolina

1 cup unsalted butter, melted

1/4 cup granulated sugar

1/4 cup rosewater or orange blossom water

Date paste or ground nuts (walnuts, pistachios, or almonds) for filling

Powdered sugar for dusting

Instructions:

In a mixing bowl, combine the semolina, melted butter, granulated sugar, and rosewater. Knead the mixture until it forms a smooth dough.

Divide the dough into small portions and shape them into balls.

Flatten each ball into a round disc, about 1/4-inch thick.

Place a small amount of date paste or ground nuts in the center of each disc.

Fold the edges of the dough over the filling, forming a sealed, decorative pattern using a ma'amoul mold or your fingers.

Place the filled cookies on a baking sheet lined with parchment paper.

Bake in a preheated oven at 350°F (175°C) for 15-20 minutes or until they are lightly golden.

Remove from the oven and let them cool completely.

Dust with powdered sugar before serving.

Origin: Ma'amoul cookies are a beloved Middle Eastern treat, often associated with festive occasions like Eid. They come in various shapes and sizes, with a variety of fillings.

Preparation Time: 30 minutes

Cooking Time: 15-20 minutes

Yield: About 24 ma'amoul cookies

Optional Variations or Substitutions: You can experiment with different fillings, such as figs, apricots, or even chocolate.

Tips and Notes for Success: Ensure the edges of the cookies are well-sealed to prevent the filling from leaking out during baking.

Mantecados (Spain)

Ingredients:

2 cups all-purpose flour

1/2 cup powdered sugar

1/2 cup lard or vegetable shortening

1/2 cup ground almonds

Zest of 1 lemon

1/2 teaspoon ground cinnamon

1/4 teaspoon ground cloves

Powdered sugar for dusting

Instructions:

Preheat your oven to 350°F (175°C). Line a baking sheet with parchment paper.

In a mixing bowl, combine the flour, powdered sugar, ground almonds, lemon zest, ground cinnamon, and ground cloves.

Add the lard or vegetable shortening to the dry ingredients. Mix until a crumbly dough forms.

Shape the dough into small, round cookies and place them on the prepared baking sheet.

Bake for 15-20 minutes or until the cookies are lightly golden.

Remove from the oven and let them cool on the baking sheet for a few minutes.

Dust the warm cookies generously with powdered sugar.

Once cooled, dust them again with powdered sugar for extra sweetness.

Origin: Mantecados are a classic Spanish Christmas cookie, especially popular in Andalusia. They are known for their crumbly texture and rich, almond flavor.

Preparation Time: 15 minutes

Cooking Time: 15-20 minutes

Yield: About 24 mantecados

Optional Variations or Substitutions: You can add a pinch of aniseed or use different spices, such as nutmeg, for variation in flavor.

Tips and Notes for Success: Handle the cookies gently, as they can crumble easily when warm. The more powdered sugar, the better!

Italian Biscotti

Ingredients:

2 1/2 cups all-purpose flour

1 1/2 cups granulated sugar

1/2 cup unsalted butter, softened

3 large eggs

1 teaspoon baking powder

1/2 teaspoon almond extract

1/2 cup whole almonds or hazelnuts

Zest of 1 lemon

Zest of 1 orange

Instructions:

Preheat your oven to 350°F (175°C). Line a baking sheet with parchment paper.

In a mixing bowl, cream together the softened butter and granulated sugar until light and fluffy.

Add the eggs one at a time, mixing well after each addition.

Stir in the almond extract, lemon zest, and orange zest.

In a separate bowl, whisk together the flour and baking powder.

Gradually add the dry ingredients to the wet ingredients, mixing until a sticky dough forms.

Fold in the whole almonds or hazelnuts.

Divide the dough into two portions and shape each into a log about 12 inches long and 2 inches wide.

Place the logs on the prepared baking sheet, leaving space between them.

Bake for 25-30 minutes or until the logs are lightly golden and firm to the touch.

Remove from the oven and let them cool for about 10 minutes.

Slice the logs diagonally into 1/2-inch-wide biscotti.

Arrange the biscotti cut-side down on the baking sheet and bake for an additional 10-15 minutes or until they are golden and crisp.

Let them cool completely on a wire rack.

Origin: Biscotti, meaning "twice-baked" in Italian, originated in the city of Prato, Italy. These crunchy, almond-flavored cookies are perfect for dipping into coffee or dessert wine.

Preparation Time: 20 minutes

Cooking Time: 40-45 minutes (including both bakes)

Yield: About 24 biscotti

Optional Variations or Substitutions: You can add dried fruits or chocolate chips to the dough for added flavor and texture. Different nut varieties can also be used.

Tips and Notes for Success: Slice the biscotti while they are still slightly warm, but allow them to cool completely for maximum crispness.

Hjónabandssaela (Iceland)

Ingredients:

1 1/2 cups all-purpose flour

1/2 cup granulated sugar

1/2 cup unsalted butter, softened

1/2 cup rolled oats

1/2 teaspoon baking powder

1/2 teaspoon ground cinnamon

1/4 teaspoon ground cardamom

1/2 cup raspberry jam (or your favorite flavor)

Powdered sugar for dusting

Instructions:

Preheat your oven to 350°F (175°C). Line a baking sheet with parchment paper.

In a mixing bowl, cream together the softened butter and granulated sugar until light and fluffy.

In a separate bowl, whisk together the flour, rolled oats, baking powder, ground cinnamon, and ground cardamom.

Gradually add the dry ingredients to the wet ingredients, mixing until a crumbly dough forms.

Press half of the dough into the bottom of the prepared baking sheet.

Spread a layer of raspberry jam evenly over the dough.

Crumble the remaining dough over the jam to create a streusel-like topping.

Bake for 25-30 minutes or until the top is golden brown.

Remove from the oven and let it cool in the pan.

Once cooled, cut into squares and dust with powdered sugar before serving.

Origin: Hjónabandssaela, which translates to "Wedded Bliss Cake," is a traditional Icelandic dessert often served at weddings. It symbolizes the sweet union of marriage.

Preparation Time: 15 minutes

Cooking Time: 25-30 minutes

Yield: About 16 squares

Optional Variations or Substitutions: You can use your favorite jam or fruit preserve for the filling. Some variations include chopped nuts or grated coconut in the topping.

Tips and Notes for Success: Be sure to allow the dessert to cool completely before cutting it into squares for neat slices.

Nankhatai (India)

Ingredients:

1 1/2 cups all-purpose flour

1/2 cup besan (chickpea flour)

1 cup ghee (clarified butter), softened

1 cup powdered sugar

1/4 teaspoon cardamom powder

1/4 teaspoon baking soda

A pinch of salt

Chopped pistachios or almonds for garnish (optional)

Instructions:

Preheat your oven to 350°F (175°C). Line a baking sheet with parchment paper.

In a mixing bowl, cream together the softened ghee and powdered sugar until light and fluffy.

Add the all-purpose flour, besan, cardamom powder, baking soda, and a pinch of salt to the ghee-sugar mixture. Mix until a soft dough forms.

Shape the dough into small balls and place them on the prepared baking sheet.

Gently flatten each ball and garnish with chopped pistachios or almonds if desired.

Bake for 15-20 minutes or until the cookies are lightly golden.

Remove from the oven and let them cool on the baking sheet for a few minutes before transferring them to a wire rack to cool completely.

Origin: Nankhatai is a traditional Indian shortbread cookie that traces its roots to the Indian subcontinent. It's known for its crumbly texture and aromatic cardamom flavor.

Preparation Time: 15 minutes

Cooking Time: 15-20 minutes

Yield: About 24 nankhatai

Optional Variations or Substitutions: You can add a pinch of saffron threads for a beautiful color and flavor. Adjust the sweetness to your liking by adding more or less powdered sugar.

Tips and Notes for Success: Handle the dough gently to avoid overworking it, which can make the cookies tough.

Speculoos (Belgium)

Ingredients:

2 cups all-purpose flour

1/2 cup unsalted butter, softened

3/4 cup brown sugar

1 egg

1/2 teaspoon baking powder

1/2 teaspoon ground cinnamon

1/4 teaspoon ground nutmeg

1/4 teaspoon ground cloves

1/4 teaspoon ground ginger

A pinch of salt

Instructions:

In a mixing bowl, cream together the softened butter and brown sugar until light and fluffy.

Add the egg and mix until well combined.

In a separate bowl, whisk together the flour, baking powder, ground spices, and a pinch of salt.

Gradually add the dry ingredients to the wet ingredients, mixing until a soft dough forms.

Shape the dough into a disk, wrap it in plastic wrap, and refrigerate for at least 1 hour or until firm.

Preheat your oven to 350°F (175°C). Line a baking sheet with parchment paper.

Roll out the chilled dough on a floured surface to about 1/4-inch thickness.

Use cookie cutters to cut out desired shapes, such as windmills or traditional speculoos designs.

Place the cookies on the prepared baking sheet.

Bake for 10-12 minutes or until the cookies are lightly golden.

Remove from the oven and let them cool on the baking sheet for a few minutes before transferring them to a wire rack to cool completely.

Origin: Speculoos, or speculaas, is a classic Belgian spiced shortcrust cookie, often enjoyed with coffee or tea. These cookies are known for their intricate designs and aromatic spices.

Preparation Time: 20 minutes (plus chilling time)

Cooking Time: 10-12 minutes

Yield: Varies depending on the size of your cookie cutters

Optional Variations or Substitutions: You can adjust the spice levels to your taste, adding more or less of the ground spices. Some recipes also use speculoos spice mix.

Tips and Notes for Success: Make sure the dough is well-chilled before rolling it out for easier handling and better cookie shapes.

Vánoční Cukroví (Czech Republic)

Ingredients:

2 1/2 cups all-purpose flour

1 cup unsalted butter, softened

1/2 cup powdered sugar

1/2 cup ground walnuts

1 egg yolk

1 teaspoon vanilla extract

Fruit preserves or jam for filling (apricot or raspberry work well)

Powdered sugar for dusting

Instructions:

In a mixing bowl, cream together the softened butter and powdered sugar until light and fluffy.

Add the egg yolk and vanilla extract, mixing until well combined.

Stir in the ground walnuts and gradually add the flour, mixing until a soft dough forms.

Divide the dough into smaller portions for easier handling.

Roll out one portion of dough on a floured surface to about 1/8-inch thickness.

Use cookie cutters to cut out various shapes.

Place half of the cut-out cookies on the prepared baking sheet.

Spread a small amount of fruit preserves or jam on each of the bottom cookies.

Top with the remaining cut-out cookies, pressing them gently to create sandwiches.

Bake for 10-12 minutes or until the cookies are lightly golden.

Remove from the oven and let them cool on the baking sheet for a few minutes before transferring them to a wire rack to cool completely.

Dust with powdered sugar before serving.

Origin: Vánoční Cukroví, or Czech Christmas Cookies, are an integral part of Czech holiday traditions. These delicate, filled cookies come in various shapes and flavors, making them a favorite during the Christmas season.

Preparation Time: 20 minutes

Cooking Time: 10-12 minutes

Yield: Varies depending on the size of your cookie cutters

Optional Variations or Substitutions: You can use different fruit preserves or jams to fill the cookies, and you can also experiment with various cookie cutter shapes for festive designs.

Tips and Notes for Success: Be sure to seal the filled cookies well to prevent the filling from leaking out during baking. Dust with powdered sugar for a beautiful presentation.

Madeleines (France)

Ingredients:

2/3 cup all-purpose flour

1/2 cup unsalted butter, melted and cooled

1/2 cup granulated sugar

2 large eggs

1 teaspoon pure vanilla extract

1/2 teaspoon baking powder

A pinch of salt

Zest of 1 lemon

Powdered sugar for dusting (optional)

Instructions:

Preheat your oven to 350°F (175°C). Grease and flour a madeleine mold or a mini muffin tin.

In a mixing bowl, whisk together the eggs, granulated sugar, and vanilla extract until pale and frothy.

In a separate bowl, sift together the flour, baking powder, and a pinch of salt.

Gently fold the dry ingredients into the egg mixture until just combined.

Stir in the melted and cooled butter until the batter is smooth.

Add the lemon zest and mix until evenly distributed.

Spoon the batter into the prepared madeleine mold, filling each cavity about 2/3 full.

Bake for 10-12 minutes or until the madeleines are golden and have a slight hump on top.

Remove from the oven and let them cool in the mold for a few minutes before transferring them to a wire rack to cool completely.

Dust with powdered sugar before serving if desired.

Origin: Madeleines are a classic French tea cake with a distinctive seashell shape. They are believed to have been created in the Lorraine region of France and gained popularity through Marcel Proust's literature.

Preparation Time: 15 minutes

Cooking Time: 10-12 minutes

Yield: About 12-16 madeleines, depending on the size of the mold

Optional Variations or Substitutions: You can add chocolate chips, ground nuts, or different citrus zest for flavor variations.

Tips and Notes for Success: It's essential not to overmix the batter to maintain the characteristic hump on the madeleines.

Polvorones (Mexico)

Ingredients:

2 cups all-purpose flour

1 cup powdered sugar

1 cup unsalted butter, softened

1/2 cup ground pecans or almonds

1/2 teaspoon ground cinnamon

1/4 teaspoon ground cloves

1/4 teaspoon anise extract (optional)

Powdered sugar for dusting

Instructions:

Preheat your oven to 325°F (160°C). Line a baking sheet with parchment paper.

In a mixing bowl, cream together the softened butter and powdered sugar until smooth.

Add the ground nuts, ground cinnamon, ground cloves, and anise extract (if using) to the butter-sugar mixture. Mix until well combined.

Gradually add the flour, mixing until a soft dough forms.

Divide the dough into small portions and shape them into round cookies or crescents.

Place the cookies on the prepared baking sheet.

Bake for 20-25 minutes or until they are lightly golden.

Remove from the oven and let them cool on the baking sheet for a few minutes before transferring them to a wire rack to cool completely.

Dust with powdered sugar before serving.

Origin: Polvorones are a traditional Mexican cookie that dates back to the colonial era. They are known for their crumbly texture and aromatic spices.

Preparation Time: 15 minutes

Cooking Time: 20-25 minutes

Yield: About 24 polvorones

Optional Variations or Substitutions: You can use different ground nuts, such as almonds or walnuts, for variety. Adjust the amount of ground spices to your taste.

Tips and Notes for Success: Handle the cookies gently when shaping them to avoid overworking the dough.

Matcha Shortbread (Japan)

Ingredients:

1 cup all-purpose flour

1/4 cup cornstarch

1 tablespoon matcha green tea powder

1/2 cup unsalted butter, softened

1/4 cup powdered sugar

1 teaspoon pure vanilla extract

A pinch of salt

Instructions:

In a mixing bowl, sift together the flour, cornstarch, and matcha green tea powder.

In a separate bowl, cream together the softened butter and powdered sugar until light and fluffy.

Stir in the vanilla extract and a pinch of salt.

Gradually add the dry ingredients to the butter mixture, mixing until a soft dough forms.

Shape the dough into a log, wrap it in plastic wrap, and refrigerate for at least 30 minutes or until firm.

Preheat your oven to 325°F (160°C). Line a baking sheet with parchment paper.

Slice the chilled dough into rounds or squares and place them on the prepared baking sheet.

Bake for 12-15 minutes or until the shortbread is lightly golden.

Remove from the oven and let the cookies cool on the baking sheet for a few minutes before transferring them to a wire rack to cool completely.

Origin: Matcha shortbread is a modern twist on traditional Japanese tea cookies. The vibrant green color and subtle bitterness of matcha make these cookies unique and delightful.

Preparation Time: 15 minutes (plus chilling time)

Cooking Time: 12-15 minutes

Yield: About 24 matcha shortbread cookies

Optional Variations or Substitutions: You can drizzle white chocolate or sprinkle additional matcha powder on top for extra flavor and decoration.

Tips and Notes for Success: Chilling the dough is essential for easy slicing and maintaining the cookie's shape.

Hertzoggies (South Africa)

Ingredients:

1 1/2 cups all-purpose flour

1/2 cup unsalted butter, softened

1/4 cup granulated sugar

2 large egg yolks

1/2 cup desiccated coconut

1/2 cup apricot jam

2 tablespoons orange juice

Grated zest of 1 orange

A pinch of salt

Icing sugar for dusting

Instructions:

Preheat your oven to 350°F (175°C). Grease a mini muffin tin.

In a mixing bowl, cream together the softened butter and granulated sugar until light and fluffy.

Add the egg yolks and mix until well combined.

Gradually add the flour, desiccated coconut, and a pinch of salt to the butter mixture, mixing until a soft dough forms.

Roll small portions of the dough into balls and press them into the greased mini muffin tin to create a tartlet shell.

In a separate bowl, mix the apricot jam, orange juice, and grated orange zest.

Spoon a small amount of the jam mixture into each tartlet shell.

Bake for 15-20 minutes or until the tartlet shells are lightly golden.

Remove from the oven and let them cool in the tin for a few minutes before transferring them to a wire rack to cool completely.

Dust with icing sugar before serving.

Origin: Hertzoggies are a classic South African cookie named after General J.B.M. Hertzog, a former Prime Minister of South Africa. They are known for their coconut-filled tartlet shells with apricot jam.

Preparation Time: 20 minutes

Cooking Time: 15-20 minutes

Yield: About 24 hertzoggies

Optional Variations or Substitutions: You can use other fruit jams or preserves, such as raspberry or strawberry, for the filling.

Tips and Notes for Success: Be sure to press the dough firmly into the mini muffin tin to create a well for the jam filling.

Almond Briouats (Morocco)

Ingredients:

1 cup ground almonds

1/4 cup powdered sugar

1 tablespoon orange blossom water

1/2 teaspoon ground cinnamon

A pinch of salt

Filo pastry sheets

Melted butter for brushing

Honey for drizzling

Toasted sesame seeds for garnish (optional)

Instructions:

In a mixing bowl, combine the ground almonds, powdered sugar, orange blossom water, ground cinnamon, and a pinch of salt to make the almond filling.

Cut the filo pastry sheets into squares or rectangles.

Take a filo sheet and brush it with melted butter.

Place a small portion of the almond filling at one end of the filo sheet.

Fold the filo sheet diagonally over the filling to create a triangle.

Continue folding the triangle until you reach the end of the sheet, brushing with more butter to seal.

Repeat with the remaining filo sheets and almond filling.

Place the briouats on a baking sheet and bake at 350°F (175°C) for 15-20 minutes or until they are golden brown.

Remove from the oven and immediately drizzle with honey and sprinkle with toasted sesame seeds if desired.

Let them cool before serving.

Origin: Briouats are a popular Moroccan pastry often made during special occasions and celebrations. These flaky, almond-filled pastries are a delightful treat with a hint of floral and nutty flavors.

Preparation Time: 20 minutes

Cooking Time: 15-20 minutes

Yield: Varies depending on the size of the briouats

Optional Variations or Substitutions: You can add finely chopped pistachios or walnuts to the almond filling for added texture.

Tips and Notes for Success: Work quickly with the filo pastry sheets to prevent them from drying out. Brushing with melted butter helps create a crispy texture.

Special Sections
Dietary Considerations:

Vegetarian Options: Many of the recipes in this cookbook are naturally vegetarian, as they rely on ingredients like flour, sugar, butter, spices, and fruits. However, please note that certain recipes may include non-vegetarian ingredients like eggs. You can often substitute eggs with egg replacers or other plant-based alternatives to make these recipes vegetarian-friendly.

Gluten-Free Options: If you or your guests have gluten intolerance or celiac disease, you can explore gluten-free flours and baking mixes available in the market as substitutes for regular all-purpose flour. Experiment with different gluten-free flours to find the one that works best for your chosen recipe. Additionally, ensure that any other ingredients you use, such as spices, flavorings, or fillings, are gluten-free.

Meal Planning:

Cookie Pairing for a Dessert Spread: Planning a festive dessert spread? Pair these Advent cookies with a variety of desserts from around the world, such as French macarons, Italian tiramisu, or Spanish churros with chocolate sauce. Create a diverse and memorable dessert experience for your guests.

Cookie Gifting: Consider gifting these homemade cookies to friends and family during the holiday season. Package them beautifully in decorative tins, boxes, or cookie bags. Attach a heartfelt note or a copy of your favorite recipe for a personal touch.

Cookie Exchange Parties: Organize a cookie exchange party with friends and neighbors. Each guest can bake a different Advent cookie from the cookbook, and everyone can exchange cookies to create a delightful assortment.

Entertaining Tips:

Themed Holiday Party: Host a themed holiday party featuring the cookies and traditions from the countries represented in the cookbook. Decorate your space with international holiday decor, play traditional music, and invite guests to dress in festive attire. Share the stories and origins of the cookies as you serve them.

Cookie Decorating Station: Set up a cookie decorating station with icing, sprinkles, and edible decorations. Allow guests, especially children, to personalize their cookies, adding an interactive and creative element to your gathering.

Hot Beverage Bar: Pair the Advent cookies with a hot beverage bar, offering a selection of teas, coffees, hot chocolates, and mulled wines from different regions. Provide garnishes like whipped cream, cinnamon sticks, and citrus slices for a festive touch.

Cookie Tasting Cards: Create tasting cards for each cookie, detailing its origin, flavor profile, and any unique traditions associated with it. Place these cards near each cookie display, allowing guests to learn about the cookies they're enjoying.

By incorporating these dietary considerations, meal planning ideas, and entertaining tips, you can elevate your cookie-baking experience and create memorable gatherings filled with the delightful flavors of Advent cookies from around the world. Enjoy sharing these delicious treats with loved ones during the holiday season and beyond.

Index

Japanese Matcha Shortbread:

Matcha Green Tea Powder

Mexican Polvorones:

Ground Pecans

Ground Cinnamon

Ground Cloves

Anise Extract (optional)

Mexican Wedding Cookies (Polvorones de Boda):

Ground Pecans

Ground Cinnamon

Powdered Sugar

Moroccan Almond Briouats:

Ground Almonds

Orange Blossom Water

Filo Pastry Sheets

Honey

Toasted Sesame Seeds (optional)

Nankhatai (India):

Ground Cardamom

Saffron Threads (optional)

ADVENT COOKIES AROUND THE WORLD: A GLOBAL GASTRONOMIC JOURNEY

Russian Tea Cakes:

Ground Nuts

Powdered Sugar

Speculoos (Belgium):

Ground Cinnamon

Ground Nutmeg

Ground Cloves

Ground Ginger

Swedish Pepparkakor:

Ground Ginger

Ground Cloves

Ground Cardamom

Traditional Mexican Conchas:

Cocoa Powder (optional)

Vanillekipferl (Austria):

Ground Hazelnuts or Almonds

Powdered Sugar

Viennese Linzer Cookies:

Ground Almonds or Hazelnuts

Raspberry Jam

Welsh Cakes:

Currants

Zimtsterne (Switzerland):

Ground Almonds

Ground Cinnamon

Lemon Zest

Use this alphabetical index to quickly find the key ingredients and corresponding recipes in the cookbook, making it easier to plan your baking sessions and explore the diverse flavors of Advent cookies from around the world.

Measurement Conversions:

Volume Measurements (US)

1 tablespoon (tbsp) = 3 teaspoons (tsp)

1 fluid ounce (fl oz) = 2 tablespoons (tbsp)

1 cup (c) = 8 fluid ounces (fl oz)

1 pint (pt) = 2 cups (c)

1 quart (qt) = 4 cups (c)

1 gallon (gal) = 4 quarts (qt)

Weight Measurements (US)

1 ounce (oz) = 28.35 grams (g)

1 pound (lb) = 16 ounces (oz)

Temperature Conversions:

Fahrenheit (°F) = Celsius (°C)

32°F = 0°C

212°F = 100°C

350°F = 175°C

Ingredient Substitutions:

Egg Substitutions:

Replace 1 egg with:

1/4 cup unsweetened applesauce - Reduces fat content

1/4 cup mashed bananas - Adds a mild banana flavor

1/4 cup yogurt or buttermilk - Adds moisture and acidity

1 tablespoon ground flaxseeds + 3 tablespoons water (let sit to thicken) - Adds a nutty flavor

Silken tofu blended until smooth - Adds creaminess

Butter Substitutions:

Replace 1 cup of butter with:

1 cup of margarine - Similar texture, but different flavor

1 cup of coconut oil - Adds a subtle coconut flavor

1 cup of vegetable shortening - Reduces flavor complexity

Flour Substitutions:

Replace 1 cup of all-purpose flour with:

1 cup of whole wheat flour - Adds a nutty flavor and more nutrients

1 cup of gluten-free flour blend - Suitable for gluten-free baking

1 cup of almond flour - Adds a nutty flavor and moisture

These conversion tables and ingredient substitutions can be valuable references while working with different measurements, temperatures, and dietary preferences in your baking adventures. They will help you adapt recipes to your specific needs and ensure successful outcomes when making Advent cookies from around the world.

Glossary - Culinary Terms:

Creaming: A baking technique where softened butter and sugar are beaten together until light and fluffy. This process incorporates air into the mixture, resulting in a tender and delicate texture in baked goods.

Sifting: The process of passing dry ingredients, such as flour or powdered sugar, through a fine sieve or sifter to break up lumps and ensure uniformity.

Zest: The outer colored part of citrus fruit (lemon, orange, lime) peel, typically grated or removed in thin strips. It adds citrusy aroma and flavor to dishes.

Egg Replacer: A substitute for eggs in recipes, often used in vegan or egg-free baking. Common egg replacers include applesauce, mashed bananas, yogurt, flaxseed meal mixed with water, silken tofu, and commercial egg replacers.

Filo Pastry (Phyllo Pastry): A thin, delicate pastry used in both sweet and savory dishes, particularly in Mediterranean and Middle Eastern cuisines. It is typically layered to create a crispy, flaky texture.

Clarified Butter: Butter from which the milk solids and water have been removed, leaving behind pure, clear butterfat. It has a higher smoke point and is often used in cooking and baking.

Confectioners' Sugar (Powdered Sugar): Finely ground sugar that is commonly used for dusting desserts, making icings, and sweetening various confections. It has a powdery texture.

Desiccated Coconut: Finely shredded, dried coconut meat that is often used in baking for its mild coconut flavor and texture.

Glossary - Ingredients:

Anise Extract: A concentrated liquid flavoring made from anise seeds. It imparts a licorice-like flavor and is used in various sweet and savory dishes.

Orange Blossom Water: A fragrant water made by distilling the blossoms of bitter orange trees. It is used in Mediterranean and Middle Eastern cuisines to flavor sweets, pastries, and beverages.

Ground Cardamom: A spice made from ground seeds of the cardamom plant. It has a sweet, floral, and slightly citrusy flavor, often used in baking and cooking.

Saffron Threads: Reddish-orange threads from the crocus flower stigma, known for their intense color and distinctive flavor. Saffron is one of the most expensive spices globally and is often used sparingly.

Ground Hazelnuts or Almonds: Finely ground nuts that are used to add flavor and texture to baked goods, such as cookies and pastries.

Currants: Small, dried, seedless grapes often used in baking for their sweet and tangy flavor. They can be added to cookies, cakes, and bread.

Ground Walnuts: Walnuts that have been finely ground into a powder. They are used to add nutty flavor and texture to various recipes.

These definitions should help readers better understand the culinary terms and ingredients encountered in the recipes from "Advent Cookies Around the World: A Global Gastronomic Journey" and make their cooking experience more enjoyable and informed.

Don't miss out!

Visit the website below and you can sign up to receive emails whenever S.R. Moore publishes a new book. There's no charge and no obligation.

https://books2read.com/r/B-A-XIBBB-TWOQC

BOOKS2READ

Connecting independent readers to independent writers.

Did you love *Advent Cookies Around the World: A Global Gastronomic Journey*? Then you should read *The Secret of Lavender Lane*[1] by S.R. Moore!

[2]

Nestled in the heart of a quaint village lies "Emma's Eats," a charming bakery known for its delectable pastries and the warm smile of its owner, Emma Thompson. But the serene life of Lavender Lane is disrupted when a mysterious book falls into Emma's hands, unearthing a trail of long-buried secrets and a forgotten tale of love and loss.

In "The Secret of Lavender Lane," the tranquility of village life intertwines with the intrigue of historical mysteries. Emma, initially just a beloved baker, finds herself at the center of a puzzling enigma that dates back generations. Along with a cast of vivid characters including

---

1. https://books2read.com/u/bzrpkn

2. https://books2read.com/u/bzrpkn

the ever-punctual Mrs. Fletcher, the knowledgeable Tom Bennett, and the spirited Lucy, Emma delves into a web of hidden pasts and concealed ties.

As the story unfolds, the discovery of cryptic symbols and hidden messages in an old recipe book sets Emma and her friends on a quest that challenges the quiet history of Lavender Lane. From the cozy confines of the bakery to the vibrant community fair, the village's charming facades and Emma's world are cast in new light, revealing the layers of history and heart that pulse beneath.

Julian Spector, a once-celebrated but now forgotten author, becomes a pivotal figure in their journey, his own secrets woven into the village's history. The quest to uncover the truth not only reveals the depth of the village's legacy but also tests the bonds of community and friendship.

"The Secret of Lavender Lane" is a tale of discovery, a celebration of the simple joys of village life, and a testament to the enduring power of stories. It's a journey through the charming streets of Lavender Lane, where every corner holds a whisper of the past, waiting to be heard. Join Emma and her friends as they unravel the mysteries of their beloved village, where every discovery is a piece of a larger, heartwarming puzzle.